The Royal Anniversary Book of Days

THE ROYAL ANNIVERSARY BOOK OF DAYS

Cecil Beaton

THE VICTORIA AND ALBERT MUSEUM

EBURY PRESS STATIONERY

First published in 1992 by Ebury Press Stationery
An imprint of the Random Century Group
Random Century House, 20 Vauxhall Bridge Road,
London SW1V 2SA

Copyright © Random Century 1992
Cecil Beaton's royal photographs © Board of Trustees,
Victoria and Albert Museum 1992

All rights reserved. No part of this book may be
reproduced in any form or by any means without permission
in writing from the publisher.

Set in Lyons Monastic and Caslon Old Face
by Alphabet, London and SX Composing, Rayleigh, Essex.

Printed in Italy

Designed by David Fordham

ISBN 0 09 177342 3

Front cover illustration: The Queen, Buckingham Palace 1955
Back cover illustration: Princess Anne, 1953
Half Title illustration: The Queen, Prince Andrew and Prince Edward, 1964
Illustration opposite title page: The Queen and the Duke of Edinburgh after the Coronation 2 June 1953

Introduction

Sir Cecil Beaton (1904-80), 'romantic Royalist' and photographer to Hollywood and *Vogue*, created a modern image of the British monarchy. Beginning in 1939, when he was first summoned to Buckingham Palace, he presented Queen Elizabeth in summer dress, hat and parasol in a sunlit garden – and his photographs were published in the illustrated press throughout Britain's then Empire. Over thirty years later he photographed the same woman, now the Queen Mother, in another garden, to conclude his series of royal portraits.

Sir Cecil Beaton renewed and revised the image of the House of Windsor for modern times. He photographed the newly crowned King George VI and Queen Elizabeth in the late 1930s and during the Second World War, when they stayed in London to share the dangers of the Blitz; he photographed the emerging princesses, Elizabeth and Margaret, the dashing Duke and Duchess of Kent and their children, most notably Princess Alexandra – one of his favourite and most inspiring models; later he photographed the families of his princesses – most notably the arrival on the stage of history of Prince Charles and Princess Anne, Prince Andrew and Prince Edward. Perhaps most nerve-wrackingly and momentously, he photographed the Coronation of Queen Elizabeth II in 1953. Eventually, in 1987, Sir Cecil Beaton's private archive of some 18,000 royal photographs was bequeathed to the Victoria and Albert Museum by Eileen Hose, his devoted secretary for over twenty years.

'I remember,' Miss Hose once wrote, 'the feeling of excitement that ran through the house when a summons was received from a Royal House to take new photographs for perhaps an anniversary, or a visit to somewhere in the Commonwealth. I could sense the intensity with which Sir Cecil was contemplating the sitting. Although there might be restrictions which would prevent his indulging totally in his imagination, and his quest for individual characteristics, his affection and warmth of feeling towards the sitter usually allowed him, he hoped, to create an image which pleased them both.'

Sir Cecil Beaton brought to royal portraiture a sense of continuity with his predecessors among the painters. As Sir Roy Strong, a former director of the Victoria and Albert Museum, friend of Sir Cecil and scholar of these portraits has written: 'To me it is Beaton's profound sense of the historic past which sets his work apart and makes it unequalled in this century by any of the photographers that preceded or followed him. Indeed, it is no exaggeration to place his work alongside that of Holbein, Velazquez or Van Dyck, for it offers a similar heady combination of art and propaganda.'

MARK HAWORTH-BOOTH,
Curator of photographs, Victoria and Albert Museum

King George VI, the Queen, Princess Elizabeth and Princess Margaret
at Windsor Castle, November 1943

~ January ~

1

2

3

4

5

6

7

PRINCESS MARGARET, 1958

CECIL BEATON

January

8

9

10

11

12

13

14

THE QUEEN, 1948

January

15

16

17

18

19

20

21

PRINCESS ALEXANDRA, APRIL 1974

January

22

23

24

25

26

27

28

PRINCE CHARLES, BUCKINGHAM PALACE 1968

CECIL BEATON

January – February

29
30
31
1
2
3
4

THE QUEEN, PRINCESS ELIZABETH AND PRINCESS MARGARET, NOVEMBER 1942

February

	5
	6
ACCESSION OF QUEEN ELIZABETH II, 1952	
	7
	8
	9
	10
	11

THE QUEEN, BUCKINGHAM PALACE 1968

~February~

12
13
14
15
16
17
18

PRINCESS MARGARET, 1949

～February～

PRINCE ANDREW, DUKE OF YORK, BORN, 1960	19
	20
	21
DUCHESS OF KENT BORN, 1933	22
	23
	24
	25

PRINCE ANDREW 1960

～February—March～

26
27
28
29
1
2
3

PRINCESS ELIZABETH, 1945

CECIL BEATON

March

4

5

6

7

8

9

PRINCE EDWARD BORN, 1964   **10**

THE QUEEN, PRINCE ANDREW AND PRINCE EDWARD, BUCKINGHAM PALACE 1964

March

11

12

13

14

15

16

17

THE QUEEN MOTHER, 1953

March

18

19

20

21

22

PRINCESS EUGENIE OF YORK BORN, 1990   **23**

24

PRINCESS MARGARET, 1949

CECIL BEATON

March

25

26

27

28

29

30

31

PRINCESS ALEXANDRA AND THE HON. ANGUS OGILVY ON THEIR ENGAGEMENT, 19 NOVEMBER 1962

CECIL BEATON

~April~

1

2

3

4

5

6

7

PRINCESS ELIZABETH, MARCH 1945

April

8

9

10

11

12

13

14

THE DUCHESS OF KENT, PRINCESS MARINA OF GREECE, BELGRAVE SQUARE 1937

April

15

16

17

18

19

20

QUEEN ELIZABETH II BORN, 1926   21

THE QUEEN 1968

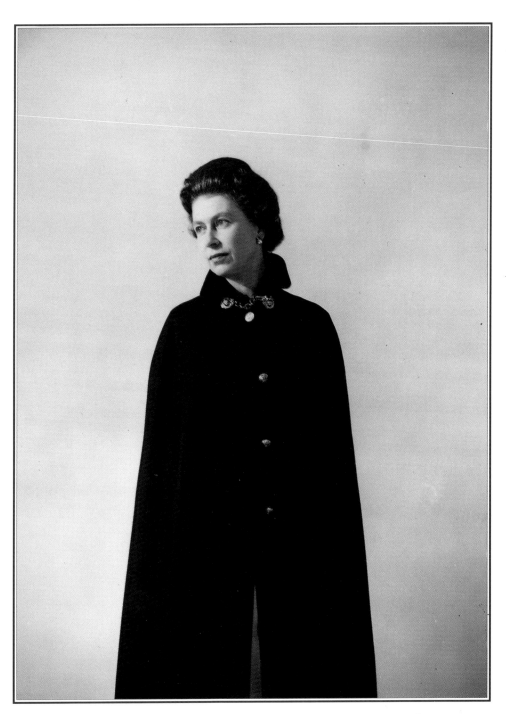

Cecil Beaton

~April~

22
23
24
25
26
27
28

QUEEN ELIZABETH 1939

~April–May~

29

30

LADY SARAH ARMSTRONG-JONES BORN, 1964   1

2

3

4

5

PRINCESS ELIZABETH AND PRINCE CHARLES, CLARENCE HOUSE SEPTEMBER 1950

CECIL BEATON

May

6
MARRIAGE OF PRINCESS MARGARET AND ANTONY ARMSTRONG-JONES, LATER THE EARL OF SNOWDON, 1960

7

8

9

10

11

12

PRINCESS MARGARET AND ANTONY ARMSTRONG-JONES ON THEIR WEDDING DAY, 6 MAY 1960

May

13

14

MISS ZARA PHILLIPS BORN, 1981   **15**

16

17

18

19

PRINCESS ELIZABETH, AGED SIXTEEN

CECIL BEATON

May

20

21

22

23

24

25

26

THE DUKE OF WINDSOR AND MRS SIMPSON, CHATEAU DE CONDE NEAR TOURS 3 JUNE 1937

Cecil Beaton

～May–June～

27

28

29

30

31

1

CORONATION OF QUEEN ELIZABETH II, 1953   2

THE QUEEN AFTER HER CORONATION, 1953

June

3

4

5

6

7

8

9

QUEEN ELIZABETH, BUCKINGHAM PALACE, JULY 1939

June

| 10 DUKE OF EDINBURGH BORN, 1921 |
| 11 |
| 12 |
| 13 |
| 14 |
| 15 |
| 16 |

THE DUKE OF EDINBURGH, 1953

~ June ~

17

18

19

DUCHESS OF GLOUCESTER BORN, 1946   20

PRINCE WILLIAM OF WALES BORN, 1982   21

22

23

PRINCESS ELIZABETH, 1945

CECIL BEATON

June

24

25

26

27

28

29

30

THE QUEEN MOTHER'S SEVENTIETH BIRTHDAY, 4 AUGUST 1970

CECIL BEATON

July

PRINCESS OF WALES BORN, 1961 INVESTITURE OF PRINCE CHARLES AS PRINCE OF WALES, 1969	1
	2
	3
PRINCE MICHAEL OF KENT BORN, 1942	4
	5
	6
	7

EDWARD, DUKE OF KENT AND PRINCE MICHAEL OF KENT, 1952

July

8

9

10

11

12

13

14

PRINCE CHARLES, BUCKINGHAM PALACE 1968

July

15

16

17

18

19

20

21

THE QUEEN AT BUCKINGHAM PALACE, 1955

Cecil Beaton

July

22

23 MARRIAGE OF THE DUKE OF YORK AND MISS SARAH FERGUSON, 1986

24

25

26

27

28

THE DUCHESS OF KENT, PRINCESS MARINA OF GREECE

July – August

MARRIAGE OF THE PRINCE OF WALES AND LADY DIANA SPENCER, 1981	29
	30
	31
	1
	2
	3
QUEEN ELIZABETH, THE QUEEN MOTHER, BORN, 1900	4

THE QUEEN MOTHER AND PRINCE CHARLES, 1953

August

5

6

7

PRINCESS BEATRICE OF YORK BORN, 1988   8

9

10

11

THE QUEEN WEARING HER ROBES AS SOVEREIGN OF THE ORDER OF THE GARTER, 1968

August

12

13

14

ANNE, THE PRINCESS ROYAL, BORN, 1950   15

16

17

18

PRINCESS ANNE, 1953

August

19

20

PRINCESS MARGARET BORN, 1930   **21**

22

23

24

25

PRINCESS MARGARET, 1956

CECIL BEATON

August–September

26	DUKE OF GLOUCESTER BORN, 1944
27	
28	
29	
30	
31	
1	

THE QUEEN AND PRINCESS ANNE, 1950

CECIL BEATON

September

2

3

4

5

6

7

8

THE QUEEN, BUCKINGHAM PALACE 1968

Cecil Beaton

September

9

10

11

12

13

14

15 PRINCE HENRY (HARRY) OF WALES BORN, 1984

PRINCE CHARLES, 1968

September

16

17

18

19

20

21

22

PRINCESS MARGARET, 1951

September

23

24

25

26

27

28

29

PRINCESS MARGARET AND THE QUEEN MOTHER, 1953

CECIL BEATON

~September—October~

30
1
2
3
4
5
6

CECIL BEATON

OCTOBER

7

8

DUKE OF KENT BORN, 1935

9

10

11

12

13

THE DUKE AND DUCHESS OF KENT ON THEIR WEDDING DAY, 8 JUNE 1961

OCTOBER

14

DUCHESS OF YORK BORN, 1959

15

16

17

18

19

20

THE QUEEN, PRINCE ANDREW AND PRINCE EDWARD, 1964

October

| 21 |
| 22 |
| 23 |
| 24 |
| 25 |
| 26 |
| 27 |

KING GEORGE VI, OCTOBER 1942

October–November

28

29

30

31

1

2

VISCOUNT LINLEY BORN, 1961
3

QUEEN ELIZABETH, 1939

Cecil Beaton

November

4

5

6

7

8

9

10

THE DUKE OF WINDSOR, 1960

Cecil Beaton

November

11

12

13

14
CHARLES, PRINCE OF WALES, BORN, 1948
MARRIAGE OF PRINCESS ANNE AND
CAPTAIN MARK PHILLIPS, 1973

15
MASTER PETER PHILLIPS BORN, 1977

16

17

PRINCE CHARLES AND PRINCESS ANNE, 1950

Cecil Beaton

November

	18
	19
MARRIAGE OF QUEEN ELIZABETH II AND THE DUKE OF EDINBURGH, 1947	20
	21
	22
	23
	24

THE QUEEN, 1955

CECIL BEATON

November—December

25
26
27
28
29
30
1

THE QUEEN MOTHER AND PRINCESS ANNE AFTER THE CORONATION, 1953

December

2

3

4

5

6

7

8

THE DUCHESS OF KENT, 1949

CECIL BEATON

~December~

9

10

11

12

13

14

15

THE QUEEN, 6 MAY 1960

CECIL BEATON

December

16

17

18

19

20

21

22

PRINCESS ELIZABETH AND PRINCE CHARLES, 1948

CECIL BEATON

December

23

24

PRINCESS ALEXANDRA BORN, 1936   **25**

26

27

28

29

PRINCESS ALEXANDRA, 1958

~December~

30

31

PRINCESS ALEXANDRA, 1959